Reflections on Poetry, Prose a

MW01295596

In this poetry book of personal reflect
journey. I especially value her answer to how we can express gratitude to God for our
blessings: "Love more, love always, live love, embrace life, and love more." If more of us
would put these words into action, our world would be in much better shape!

> Gerald Corey, Ed.D., ABPP
> Professor Emeritus of Human
> Services and Counseling
> California State University, Fullerton

Doctor Kellie Kirksey speaks with the inimitable voice of the heart. Her words emerge,
like someone who has taken a long dive into the depths of the ocean, jubilant and
powerful, clutching the precious pearl of a wisdom that is lived. Let Dr. Kirksey's words
rest in a deep place within your heart.

> Scarlet Soriano, MD
> Integrative Medicine Physician
> Health and Wellness Consultant
> Boston Medical Center

Dr. Kirksey's poetic words are like still waters that bless the soul and raging rivers that
challenge the mind.

> Carmella Marie Williams
> Kitchen Chemist
> Creator/Founder of Carmella
> Marie Natural Hair Care Products

"Poetry, Prose and Miscellaneous Musings is full of spiritual and emotional journeys. It's
also a destination where we find love, God and our best selves in the most authentically
human and beautifully messy way."

> Marlie Hall, News Anchor

Poetry, Prose and Miscellaneous Musings

Volume I

Dr. Kellie N. Kirksey

Library of Congress Control Number:		2011907155
ISBN:	Hardcover	978-1-4628-6786-8
	Softcover	978-1-4628-6785-1
	eBook	978-1-4628-6787-5

Print information available on the last page.

Rev. date: 08/24/2018

To order additional copies of this book, contact:
Xlibris
1-888-795-4274
www.Xlibris.com
Orders@Xlibris.com
547512

Dedication

To my parents Annette and Hank Kirksey. To my husband Cesar Augustin and to my children Kelsie, Dominic and Gabrielle who have all encouraged, inspired and graced me with unconditional love and support.

Honoring our Dreams

I have always dreamed of writing books. My mind works in terms of the stories that I see taking shape in my life. We all have a book within us that needs to be written. Some books are for the masses and some are just for us.

This volume represents a resounding 'yes' to my dream of writing. This is a project of permission giving. There is so much healing power in the expression of our personal narrative. My writing has always poured onto napkins, or the backs of envelopes in a desperate handwriting that even I sometimes cannot understand. Writers have to free their words; if not for others then certainly for themselves.

I spoke at a conference once and told the audience that as writers we have an obligation to release the elixir from our souls. We may be the divine vessel through which someone's medicine flows. I knew my words were a truth that I had personally experienced on many occasions. I have been consistently transformed by the words of my teachers and encouragers: Dr. Maya Angelou, Nikki Giovanni, Khalil Gibran, Rumi, Hafiz, and of course Langston Hughs. I asked myself did I truly have the courage to release my poetry into the world. Would I live the life of a dream deferred, or lament that life for me ain't been no crystal staircase? Could I actually have courage enough to bring forth the multitude of hibernating books in my soul?

At some point I had to stop talking about what I was going to do and simply allow myself the freedom to speak life and truth as I perceive it. Marianne Corey is the woman who issued a most powerful challenge. She walked up to me after a presentation and looked into my eyes. No smile. Just still, clear eyes. In a low voice, she simply said, "tell your truth." I was surprised because this woman is a strong woman of few words. When she speaks, it is meaningful and has depth. I left the conference and wondered, "When will I have the courage to share my stories?"

This first book is a compilation of my journeys. These musings are pulled from the pages of my journals, which have been faithful friends since the age of 10 or so.

Some of the journeys involve travel to faraway continents, while others speak to the journey to the interior of my soul.

Thank you for sharing a bit of my freedom-song. Now is the perfect time to manifest your dreams. May blessings and miracles abound in your life and may you give wings to the secret desires of your heart.

Peace.

Dr. Kellie

The Spiral of life involves going in and Coming Out. Be not afraid to linger where your Soul begs you to reside. There is great purpose in all the seasons of our earthly existence. Activate your purpose by breathing into the tight spaces in your life. Allow the Presence of the Great I AM to heal your illusion of lack. We are not alone. We are ALL One. Activate your Purpose Now.

Journey Series

1.

Life is a series of journeys . . . .
Some
begin anew,

Some
pick up where they left off,

Some
simply are eternal,

Never ending,

Always existing.

Embrace Life

The infinite Journey.

2.

When
I stopped looking
For what I Thought I needed,
I took a breath and Joy rose up.
She wrapped her warm arms around me.
and whispered, "You are not Alone."

3.

I am my beloved safe space

4.

I forgave myself
Again,
Again and again
Until I believed it . . .
And only then was I set free.

5.

The journey was long;
I took a car, a bus, a ferry, a taxi.
No money in my pocket
Yearning to see the unseen
Eagerly waiting to touch
The place of my longing.
Deep anticipation and
fear as the cement bench gave
me a sacred slumber
under a blanket of stars.
waiting for daylight and
a blessed pilgrimage to the motherland.

6.

It is your time
to journey to the center of yourself;
to heal your life from past hurt,
in a way that is supportive,
intentional, and self-empowering.
It is your time to journey home.

7.

The
rain
sizzled
around
my feet
. . . I ran like the wind,
Drenched
and
exhilarated
the journey consumed all of me.

8.

I lamented my journey
                until I looked back
                and remembered
                        all the laughter along the way.

9.

Donde voy yo?
No tengo idea,
pero
me voy en paz.

10.

Cyber Café.
Eyes staring at pixels.
Disconnected from
the
human embrace.
Journeying through
the web of society.
Sitting with mocha java and hot isolation.

11.

Oh how I wish my friend had lived to see
his journey through to the end.
Yet, Who am I to know when someone's journey
has come to a natural close?
My humanity grieves, yet my soul is grateful for time spent
together
I give thanks for our shared journey.
The travels, the laughs, the dancing, the tears.
Our soul's connection is eternal.
Journey on in peace, my friend.
Until we meet again.

12.

Sometimes
I
simply yearn
to journey in

solitude.

Just the wind and me.

13.

I took a journey on Memorial Day.
To the house of my fears.
Where the rats as big as cats claimed space.
Where the cold pierced the pipes and the thieves
visited when they pleased.
So there was the porch my mom jumped from.
There was the other porch I fell from. Nose scraped clean.
Wounded on the left side, no one knew but me.
It didn't bleed. It just hurt deep to the bone.
I journeyed back to the house of abuse mingled with
love . . . you know, I saw flowers on the steps,
folks grilling on the porch
no one breaking down the front door.

The journey back told me a tale.
Wake up, sleeping scared child.
The house is just a house.
Now is a perfect time to awaken from your
nightmare and choose to live.

14.

Mama Nim
She baked the best sweet potato pie.
Some said her pound cake was unforgettable.
We would taste of it baby
Love stirred in all of it
Oxtail soup and greens from the garden.

You could set a tray on her tail,
No one could beat the way she swayed.
Stopping traffic with her Caddi.
Keeping a steady gait
Checking on da folk up the street
Stopping at the Tasty Freeze.

It don't get no betta than that;
Anybody that loved us
Mama loved them too.

Anybody that needed a place, had a place.
Pops in the basement
Miss Minnie in the backroom
Gia upstairs.

Everyday ain't Sunday
But God is good.
Ain't no nutha Mama
It is what it is
And Thank God for what it is.
We can't go back, She has gone to glory
But how blessed are we
To have had Momma an Nim.

February 3, 2011

The Answer

She asked her
Afro wearing,
hip swinging,
doctorate getting,
licensed, certified and sanctified self . . . .

"When would she arrive at the sacred land called
enoughness?"

The Great I Am smiled and replied,
"Oh my wild child,
You will be enough
when you say it is so"

Believe it with every strand of your Divine DNA.
I created you as perfectly Enough.
You chose to relinquish your true self.
Now sit and reflect doctor . . . .
Drink your own elixir.

I rise above
my day to day.
Breathe, Observe, Reflect.
And so it is.
All my moments unfold as Miracles.
My life is a tapestry of Ministry.

What is Peace

Walk in the Light of Joy.
Dance the Dance of Happiness.
Sing the song of Peace
And Love.

By G.A. 4/16/09

To the Group Leaders from Spring 2008

Applause for your ability to show up . . .
To share, to look inward,
To be transparent.
Applause for the inner struggle and the courage
To try new things.
Applause for taking the Lead,
Trying on a new hat,
Going into the unknown.
I have been energized by your light.
Encouraged by your integrity
And thankful to have shared this space and time.
My prayer for you, is that you would step into your role as leader.
Trusting God to support you in all ways, at all times.

Self-loathing
slays the gentle heart.
Unworthiness
strips our humanity.
It propels us into an early grave.
Choose Life . . . Choose Love.

How do I thank God for my blessings?
Love More
Love Always
Live Love
Embrace Life
Love More!

God, I am joyful
and I am sad . . .
all at once.
There it is . . .
grieving and living.
I cannot do without your beautiful guidance,
It is a golden thread that stitches me together.
I love you Lord and thank you for it all.

We
must
keep
our hearts
forever pliable:
Open to new pathways and promise.

Miracles abound . . .
Even as challenges
and
sadness crowd our days . . .
It is all part of life-stuff.
Notice it
and
step forward anyway.

Our painful history
eats us whole for breakfast,
Renders us unconscious.
Stuck in worn-out patterns from yesteryear.
Lost in non-living.
Wake up!

Que hago yo?
Quiero sentirme mejor.
Estoy rezando.
Quiero volar!

We can talk
And
teach about the doing,
But
we must endeavor to demonstrate and act
For real change to happen.

Thinking of Cesar

He bought me a gift:
A beautiful dress
Black, with a skirt that whirled
. . . and a delicate embroidered hem.
The thin shoulder straps
Holding the gift in place.
The gift of being known, loved, and recognized.
For me . . . an invitation to embrace love.
An invitation
To dance in red shoes with my beloved.
4/26/08

It's a Hair Thing

I could feel her knees pressing into my rib cage as I sat on the flour canister getting my hair pressed.

The house would smell like burned hair even before the comb would touch a single strand.

The hot comb was well-seasoned.

Black and heavy,

with teeth close together and a sheen of grease melded into it, the handle was burned in places but you could still see the original royal blue wooden handle.

Mama's hot comb had tamed millions of strands of hair and had converted a multitude of Afros.

I was probably four or five years-old when I first got to line up with the sisters for a good hard pressing by Mama . . . it was a holiday thing.

All four of us girls and my cousins would usually be in the lineup to transform our wire-like tresses on the same day.

You know it had to be a special occasion to line up six girls and press, grease, curl, twirl, and roll (sometimes on the pink sponge rollers and sometimes on strips of folded brown paper bags)!

There was something comforting about getting my hair pressed.

I could feel the heat from the stove and the warmth from Mama's body all at once.

I would lean back against her soft body when she pressed the front of my hair . . . it felt like a hug and I knew that I was a part of the pressing club (and Mama pressed like no one else). Mama was tough but gentle with a hot comb.

She never hit me in the head with the comb for making a move like my older sister did, but I did have my share of hair pressing injuries.

The grease would sizzle and scald my head; I would let out a loud, "Ouch!" and she would never fail to say, "Mama didn't burn you, it was just the grease."

"Ok, Mama" I'd say, and then resume my posture of being as still as a statue.

Mama was a professional at pressing hair, and pressing clothes (she could put a crease in a pair of jeans that could cut you!).

We would be lined up to get the hair fried and once we got off the pressing seat, it was straight to the mirror . . . smiling in the mirror at our flowing hair . . .

no more gnarled braids and nappy kitchens (the hair at the nape of the neck that reverts from straight to kinky first, or goes back to Africa as I like to say).

All was not glory in the land of pressed hair.

Pressed hair, temporary straight hair, fried hair, it came with a price.

You could not sweat, swim, go out in the rain, sauna, or meet moisture in any way, or your tresses would return to Africa faster than you could shake a stick.

When hair is pressed, there must be no excess activities (it makes me wonder about the number of things I did or did not do for the sake of straight hair!).

When I was 22 years-old I got my first relaxer.

My hair was chemically straightened for the first time . . . no more hot comb . . . the end of an era.

I had spent most of my college years getting my hair pressed by my friend on a hot plate in the bathroom.

I was hesitant to make this drastic move to a chemical straightener but by this time Mama had a relaxer and said it was time for me to make the move.

So I followed Mama's lead.

By the time I was 29 I had my first child.

I had prayed for a son because I knew nothing about combing a little girl's hair.

I, of course, gave birth to a beautiful baby girl with a head full of hair.

For the first year of her life my mom wondered why her hair didn't grow.

Well, it grew alright, but I kept it trimmed nicely.

Eventually, I began to let my relaxer grow out, because I realized that I had been away from the hair texture that God gave me for so long, and that I had no idea how to work with my daughter's natural hair.

It was sad.

I have had natural hair for about 22 years now.

I am happy and nappy. It is really a love thing.

I have decided to just love the hair that God gave me and have fun with it.

I usually wear my hair in double strand twist, which some affectionately call, "contemporary dread locks."

I do get my hair flat ironed on occasion . . . it just depends on my mood, season and flow of life.

Usually in the spring and summer, I just rock my 'fro.

I wake up, shower, slather on some miscellaneous moisture, sometimes olive oil, and I go play in the rain or head to my next adventure.

I do my natural thing, just as God intended me to do . . . and it feels good.

I no longer beat my hair into straight submission . . . unless I am feeling straight and laced that day.

It is all a choice.

Natural hair is my fun choice.

I am more of who I am . . . and I smile to myself because it is all good.

When my seven year-old Gabrielle saw that my hair was suddenly straight one day . . . guess what happened? She asked to get her hair straightened also.

I agreed and took her down to Miss B's house.

My child came home with all kinds of hair flowing down her back.

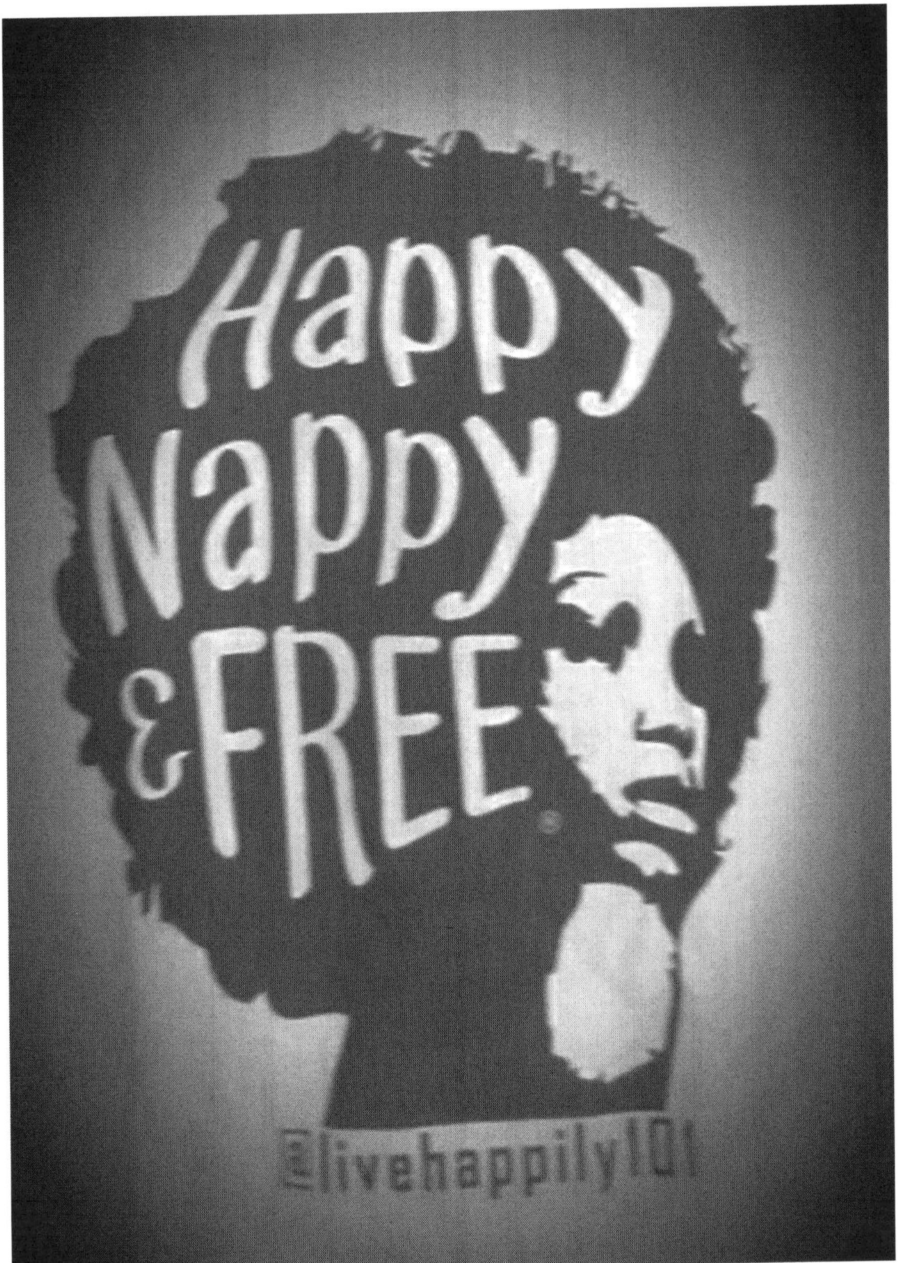
Happy
Nappy
&FREE
@livehappily101

I was in shock and fear. It was lovely, but I thought, "how in the world am I going to keep that hair tamed?"

I began to grease it, roll it up and tie it at night.

In the morning, the scarf would be on the floor, the rollers under the bed, and hair all over her head.

I was tired of trying to keep the hair decent.

Doing hair was not my gift.

Gabrielle would cry when I combed it, and she would come home from school looking a bit crazy about the head.

One morning, Gabrielle came up to me and said, "Mom, I'm tired of doing my hair everyday, can I get twists again?" I said, "You and me both!"

We both headed off to get our hair twisted again.

We did not have time for hair styles to dictate our activities . . . we valued our time and peace a lot more.

So, today we are both nappy and happy, proud of our hair texture and refusing to beat it and heat it into submission.

We choose to just simply let it be!

Naps and all!

Monday, June 21, 2010
For Real?

Many days in my life transpire like a movie.

I ask myself, did that just happen?

*I ponder, is this life of mine simply a hologram of
events that I have construed to heal my soul?*

*I write my days and journal my nights;
life is extraordinary in every single way.*

*I am constantly amazed by the synchronicities of life
which I refuse to label as chance encounters.*

Each moment is a sacred dance . . . . even this one.

Wednesday, May 5, 2010
Always in Movement

I find myself moving at the speed of light.

Filling my days with fancy and folly.

The frenzy becomes a haze, which becomes a spiral . . . . a downward whirling, and then I crash.

I lay lifeless in a heap wondering what went wrong, how did I end up in this space of nothingness . . . devoid of energy, drive, and desire, barely recognizing myself.

I was deaf to the language of my movements.
The other day as I sat on a swing, moving forward and back, I realized that I was holding on so tightly that my hands were actually throbbing.

With this new awareness I decided to loosen my grip, less redundancy . . . . what could happen?

I let up a bit and realized that I was not being hurled from the swing . . . .

I was simply moving forward and back and not experiencing discomfort in my hands . . . .
I loosened up and still I was safe. It was a new concept . . . .

later in the day I was able to sit by the pond, breathing, and resting.

My trajectory had shifted,

greater awareness had been ignited . . . .

my movement slowed for an instance and for a moment I was held softly in a blanket of peace.

Posted by kalico at *9:06 PM 0 comments* ✐
Labels: *awareness, energy, swinging*

Saturday, May 1, 2010

Cooking in the DARK

I remember when I went to turn on my kitchen light and it didn't work.

I asked a guy over to fix it and he couldn't figure out what was wrong with it.

I took a lamp and put it on my kitchen table . . . . the table I bought off of the street in Cleveland about 16 years ago.
The table with the mismatched chairs.

I just sat the lamp there and for the next 7 years I did not have a working light in my kitchen.
It never dawned on me that I could just run up to Home Depot and buy a ceiling light and get someone to install it.
No, I just dealt with my lightless circumstances as if it were normal.

Back in March I invited some ladies over from the church.
They asked where my light switch was, where my microwave
was, where was my this and my that.
I cupped my hand over my mouth like a megaphone and stated,
"attention ladies, I do not have a working light or a microwave
that works,
I don't know where anything is because nothing in my house
has a home.

I stuff things anywhere, so just go in the attic or the basement
or anywhere and look for what you need because I don't know
where anything is.

So ladies, make yourself at home."

When the words fell out of my mouth, I realized that crazy had
come to visit.

Here I was, a doctor, married to a doctor, with no light in my
kitchen and a crazy, rickety kitchen table. So what was wrong
with this picture?

I realized that I did not think I deserved more . . . I settled for
whatever was present.

The very next week, I bought a raffle ticket from my church . . .
it cost $100.00;

I prayed before I picked the ticket.

I asked God to guide me to the winning ticket.

I left the church and took the kids to volunteer at the Catholic Worker house.

We had a great time and finished up in time to get to the St.Patrick's dinner where the raffle winners would be announced by the Mayor of our town.

I told the people at my table that I was going to win.

As God is my witness, my name was called for the 2nd place winner.

I won $4000.

The next day I bought a light and donated money to the church . . . . no more cooking in the dark.

The LIGHT was now on . . . . and I came home to myself.

Praise be to God!!!!!
Posted by kalico at *7:51 AM 0 comments* ✐
Labels: *faith, light, raffle*

Friday, April 30, 2010
Flow

These days I walk in a synchronicity that I am keenly aware of.
I follow my internal inclination to speak, stop, move, and act.
For so long I have wrestled with myself.
I played hide-and-seek with me, often not knowing if I was coming or going.
My daughter asked me yesterday what it felt like to change lives.
I told her that I did not know that I was changing lives.
I pray that I am.
Sometimes I feel crazy and blessed all at the same time.
Posted by kalico at 5:14 AM 0 comments 🖉
Labels: Flow

Sunday, April 25, 2010
Wake up!

Life everyday is like a series of links.

Everything impacts everything else.

It's as if I can actually see the thread weaving life together.

It is odd and scary and joyful all at once.

I am not sure what my mission is, but I know something amazing is happening.

I went to a conference a few weeks ago and wandered into a reception.

Once in the crowded room I spotted a beautiful woman in a simple elegant black dress. she stood up and began to sing with the band . . . . the song only had 2 words . . . . WAKE UP . . . . over and over in a haunting melody she crooned the words . . . . WAKE UP.

Somehow I knew she was talking to me.

The Land of Love

A wise man once told me that when you are courting,
You and your beloved reside in Sweet Land.
A place where music and poetry and proclamations of
Tender love are professed as often as the respiration of one's breath.
Once a couple has taken a vow of holy matrimony
They walk together from Sweet Land, to the land of Complications.
How does a marriage survive The Land of Complications, I asked?
He replied, "Marriage in the Land of Complications only survives
When the couple is sealed together by a common belief in a
God that is bigger than themselves.
The couple must be firmly anchored in their eternal
commitment of life and love together.
The Land of Complications is far easier to survive when the
love between a couple surpasses the storms of life. As we know,
the storms will come.
A couple must hold fast to the treasures exchanged between
two sweet hearts.
The days of yesteryear are always close at hand when the
symphony of Sweet Land continues to ring softly in
Their hearts and the security and sweetness of a
Gentle kiss and warm embrace is never far."

Inspired by the Love of:
Janine Gibbs Augustin
et
Dr. Cesar Augustin

The April 2009 series

alcohol
sharp words,
slaps and pulled hair.
Weapons in the war without uniforms.

So they called her
brazen,
Wild woman
of the night.
So blind are they.
Unable to see
that her true passion, was her God

There she was.
Moving as if in a trance.
She danced her deep pain.
Twirling until she could live again.

Who
knew
The drum
was her survival place.
The heart still beats as it bleeds.

In
a breath
Yesterday rose up
like an angry tidal wave.
Smashing all in her wake . . . . Fighting for her life.

Am I still breathing?
This moment
feels so sacred.
So miraculous.
God?
have I ascended?

My Past
Tightly woven into my physiology.
Present moment awareness has no room to breathe.
A silent death to conscious living.

How do we begin to free the things that bind us?
How can we deconstruct without undoing ourselves?
How can we push through all the dark places and live?
. . . Say yes to the partnership of fear and faith.
Dance with the Fear you ran from.
Choose life in all her phases.

I say yes to confronting my own stuff.
I need to just do it.
Pain and all.
I must stay on the path to my well being,
even though my feet burn hot on the coals of life . . .
I will not turn and run.
I will face her with courage and a prayer.

Women and Dreams

Women who Endeavor To revisit their Dreams
Radiate Passion, Courage, and Zest for life.
Their vibration stirs the soul of those around them.
It moves from sister to sister in a subtle rhythm of hope and
determination.
The energy rises up from the spine and out through the
crown as a transparent halo.
Entranced are those who encounter women who revisit
abandoned dreams.
Inspired, Encouraged and Awakened,
Observers become the Doers, and the legacy continues.
Women Revisiting, Embracing, Living their dormant dreams
become as sacred as
The earth we walk on.
Ashay, Amen
Honor Your Dreams

Try

My father always said to me,
"Nothing Beats
A Failure
But a try."
In my youth I was never quite sure what this meant.
As I grew older and watched my father go from the bar
business, to the restaurant business, to travel, to transmission,
to fast food, to beauty shop, to realty etc.
I grew to learn what this phrase meant
Dad lived this phrase.
You never know your potential in life if you never try.
The only thing that can challenge a perceived failure is a
try, an effort, a movement in the direction of one's dreams,
hopes, and inclinations.
I echo the words of my father to my children.
I let them see me do the things that are off the beaten path,
challenging, and worthwhile to my spirit.
It is in our Trying, Falling, and Doing that we encourage
ourselves and all our relations to be more than we ever
dreamed we could be.
Failure is simply an experience when one summons the
courage to Try.

Keep Dreaming

Upon the birth of my first child, I lay in the hospital bed,
pain running through my post-cesarean body. My ache was
outweighed only by my euphoric joy of having co-created with
the Divine.
My little perfect girl with eyes of wisdom felt like my entire
world. My whole self embraced this little person. What a
precious gift. How blessed was I?
My mother observed me and smiled gently at my beautiful
little girl with the bright brown eyes.
Slowly my mom walked over to my bed and came very close to
my left side. She leaned in and whispered in my ear. I could
feel her warm breath.
This is what she said, "I know that right now you feel your
daughter is your entire world, but one day she will be grown
and will leave your house. You will have to live your separate
life. Do not ever forget your dreams, hold on to them and live
them. Love your little girl, but keep living your dreams. You
may not understand this now, it may sound harsh, but one
day you will understand."
The wisdom of our elder's show up in subtle whispers in the
midst of life.
Remember the mother wit; embrace the sage woman who,
inspired by the Divine, delivers messages for resiliency and
guidance for your many journeys in life.
Stay Alert, Stay Aware, Stay Present
Keep your dreams
Live your dreams
Give your dreams
a Vibrant Life.

Oh Oneness

We walked
Side by Side
All the Days
Of my life,
Yet I ran Ahead
So fast, so far, neglecting to absorb the brilliance of your
Divine unconditional love.
Now as I walk in this season of death and Resurrection,
I am fully awake to your loving kindness.
It is only now that my life has begun to unfold the true
Spiritual assignment
my soul said yes to.
Living the pain, bruised, and triumphant.
Standing as a witness~a testimony to grace and miracles. It is
only today that I live into the Dream.
that you breathed into me
on the day my soul was born.

God
Guide me.
In all things
In Everything.
There is no
Dwelling Place
Where you are not Present.
I Adore Thee.

If it were not for prayer, I could not breathe
I could not live.

My Lord.
How good it is to know that I do not walk this earth alone.
Sometimes the journey feels like thorns on my back;
and then I am reminded that even to feel the piercing thorns
is a prayer I can offer to the Divine.

I refuse to be bitter.
To be bitter is a choice.
To forgive is a gift we bestow upon ourselves.
To release the taste of stagnant anger
is to consciously create space for Divinity in our Spirit.
Make intentional room for the Best.

I surrender.
I surrender.
I can change
Nothing!
So where to from here?
Where do I begin?
How do I begin anew?
Lord
I surrender.

Oh God
Oh God
Why did I shelter myself from you.
Shivering and sweating under covers
I hid myself in my pain.

Why did I hide? When you were there, sitting next to me,
waiting?

Did I not believe that you created the very essence of me?
Why shiver when the arms of the Lord our God are so warm
and comforting.
Why do we reject that which has come for our deep healing?

Stop the mad Searching

I woke up late for church today.
I wanted to see my people, but my body was feeling
resistant and achy.
I just surrendered to the feeling and slowly pulled myself
together and got dressed.
The cross that my father had bought me years ago was on my
mind and I thought well, I'm not going to church, I may as
well wear that sparkly cross.
The one dad gave my sister Tracey and I on our birthday so
long ago.
I remember him pulling two crosses out of the gift area on the
back porch.
I really thought to myself, here goes dad giving her the best again.
My sparkly tacky cross didn't suit my personality.
Over the years I began to love this cross. I wore it
everywhere . . . South Africa, Senegal, Spain.
It just became a part of me and it became this connection
with my wild and yet compassionate dad.
I loved the way it sparkled in the world . . . it blessed me and
reminded me of family and crazy jaunts in life.
So this morning I woke up in my same junky room.
Stuff all over the place.
Feeling my cross, and of course not knowing where the heck it was.
Here I go again spinning tail into oblivion.
Judging my mess and cursing myself for continuing the habit
of dropping my stuff wherever it wanted to go
(usually into a heap somewhere).

I tore things up even more.
Where was my cross?
I wanted It.
I needed it.
No other accessory would do.
I mean, it is the 4th week of lent and all.
I have not given up enough or transformed enough.
Couldn't I at least wear my sparkly cross?
It seemed so childish that I passed the minutes searching
instead of living. Judging myself for what I wasn't,
instead of embracing who I am.
I mean, why the tirade because I could not find my cross, or
my right career, or my soul's purpose, or my soul mate, or my
best most impassioned this or that?
Always a fricking excuse for being not enough.
Always desperately seeking that thing that would make me
whole and sparkly and happy and transformed and elevated
and all those words we love to say: I really think I am junk,
and when I find the right key, I will be joyful beyond my own
understanding.
What would happen if I stopped my mad quest for that thing
that would change my existence?
Would I fade away if I relinquished my mission . . . my search?
I have spent a lifetime in search of that holy grail of
ultimate healing.
Chasing the right medicine has been a quest.
What would make me the best counselor, professor, mother,
wife, friend, student? The workshops, certifications, and
techniques blurred together like the pile of clothes and tangle
of costume jewelry and papers sprawled out on my
dresser and floor.

Searching . . . judging, passing time in a space of "please God
save me from this self that I am."
The sun began to shine, my family would be back
from church soon.
All ready to head to lunch, then off to Cleveland to do taxes
with miracle man cousin Sonny.
Forget the cross.
I was just satisfied (or so I told myself) to have found my
passport and the sweater I wanted to wear.
I stared at the mess and began to make my bed, neaten my
stacks, and put my jewelry back into semi order (not really).
I went to close my jewelry box and something told me to move
one more thing to the side. There it was, my chainless cross.
I was so surprised.
It was as if the angels placed it there and said, "look girl,
there you go again looking so hard that you can't find what's
staring you in the face.
I pulled a chain off of another necklace and put my cross on.
It's a bit worn and its leaning to the side a bit.
Even the cross has a flawed character that I love and embrace.
So what about me?
Can I embrace the parts of me that are rough, imperfect and
leaning to the side a bit?
Can I love on all those jagged edges?
What if I focused on the accepting instead of the medicine
that would heal me of my divine imperfect self?
What if I could just love me to amazing grace
(one of my mom's favorite sayings)?
What if I could stop searching, be still, and bump into myself
in those unexpected sweet moments?
I look back on my life and if I connected all the dots

the truth is that I happened upon my joy when I least
expected it.
The connections were made without my interference.
people and information flowed
to me at the right time.
I look at some of my tribe (those people that know the soul of
me from a time when we walked through life together, making
agreement to always stand for each other in this life and
beyond), and remember the ways we encountered each other.
We did not encounter each other in the searching but in the
living of my day to day moments.
One was my neighbor, one a student, one a teacher, one a
friend . . . a sister . . . a communion giver, a pediatrician, a
therapist.
All mingling together in my everyday life,
The unexplainable happenstance of existence:
It's beautiful and effortless.
I endeavor to stop making my life a mad search for
truth and wholeness.
I endeavor to live my life in mundane and amazing ways,
letting my journey unfold before me as the gift that it is.
My search is for this moment; in my humanity I will surely
forget again and someone or something or some song will
remind me who i am Again. I get on with the living of my
true life.
I am my safe space.
I am my divine compass.
The search is over
. . . and so it is for this moment.

Dr. Kirksey Dreaming Awake at the Oprah Winfrey Live the Life You Want Tour in Detroit. This was my dream reactivation weekend! 9/12/14

Go Wake up your Sleeping Dreams and post them at Happynappy&free on Facebook. Nappy is a State of Radical Self LOVE regardless of age, race, gender, political view, sexual orientation, religion, culture etc. Nappy=Self love Right Now!@ livehappily101

visit www.drkelliek.com

Tell your story

Tell your story

This is My Truth

This is My Truth

This is My Truth

This is My Truth

This is My Truth

This is My Truth